A HEART LIKE JESUS

A REGNUM CHRISTI ESSAY ON CONTEMPLATING AND IMITATING JESUS

FR. JOHN BULLOCK, LC

TABLE OF CONTENTS

INTRODUCTION 5

THE HUMAN HEART AND ITS LONGING
FOR LOVE AND INTERIOR PEACE 9

What Is the Heart? What Is Love? 10

Our Heart's Longings for Love and Peace 12

To Be Loved...13

To Love...14

Interior Peace 15

Interior Peace and Love Are Mutually Beneficial............... 18

All Our Desires Point to God and
Prepare Us to Encounter Him 19

Discussion Questions 20

ATTRIBUTES OF JESUS'S HEART 21

Five Attributes of the Heart of Jesus................................... 25

Equanimity.. 26

Emotional Richness 28

Affection 29

Self-Assuredness 32

Passion.. 33

The Two Loves Which Unify All of Jesus's Endeavors 34

Jesus as Model of the Integral Heart................................... 36

Discussion Questions.. 37

PUTTING ON THE HEART OF JESUS 39

Reliance upon Grace 39

Collaboration with Grace 41

Perseverance 43

Discussion Questions 45

CONCLUSION: 46

EPILOGUE: 50

Backstory 51

Who Is Jesus for Me? 53

ENDNOTES 56

INTRODUCTION: CLOTHE OURSELVES WITH THE HEART OF JESUS

"Set me as a seal upon your heart, as a seal upon your arm; For Love is strong as Death, longing is fierce as Sheol. Its arrows are arrows of fire, flames of the divine. Deep waters cannot quench love, nor rivers sweep it away. Were one to offer all the wealth of his house for love, he would be utterly despised"
Song of Songs 8:6-7

Like arrows of fire, true love brings pain, but also profound joy. Love is all-consuming. It longs for an inseparable union with the beloved, "as a seal upon your heart." This passage from the Song of Songs describes our longing for human and divine love. It also describes the intensity of God's love for us.

Through the miracle of the Incarnation, God came to love man with a human heart, his Sacred Heart. Everything Our Lord did in his earthly life was an expression of his all-consuming love for us, "For God so loved the world that he gave his only Son, so that everyone who believes in him might not perish but might have eternal life."[1] His passion, death, and resurrection proved that his love is not merely "strong as Death," but stronger.

Faced with such a love, our only legitimate response is to love with an equal intensity. To offer anything less, even "all the wealth of [our] house… would [merit to] be utterly despised." However, even if we were to respond with all our love, and nothing but love, we would still fall short. That is why the first fruit of Our Lord's redemption was "God's love poured into our hearts through the Holy Spirit who has been given to us."[2] Therefore, with the very Spirit of God animating our actions we are empowered to love more worthily.

Nevertheless, baptism, through which we receive the Holy Spirit, is only the beginning of a journey. The seed planted in our souls must grow. God's grace elevates our nature; it does not replace it. We must grow in love.

The Regnum Christi Statutes state that our ideal is to proclaim and expand Christ's kingdom by seeking to "clothe ourselves with Christ in our hearts and in our works, so he reigns in our lives through a progressive configuration with him."[3] Therefore, our very purpose as Regnum Christi members, as Christians, is to have a heart like Jesus.[4]

Getting there is a process.

How do we do that? We must know our own heart, the heart of Jesus, and some principles for the journey. However, each of these three topics is vast. To narrow our focus, we shall concentrate on a perspective that is proper, but not exclusive, to Regnum Christi: the integral, or harmonious, understanding of the human heart and its vocation to love. We desire, and Jesus possesses, a harmony within the heart. It is this harmony, or peace, between our intellect, will, emotions, and appetites that enables us to love more perfectly. Therefore, this essay will:

1. Reflect upon the human heart and its longing for love and interior peace.

2. Contemplate some attributes of the heart of Jesus which reflect his passionate love and interior harmony.

3. Offer some concrete principles to assist in our effort to "put on" Christ in our hearts.

Finally, it will conclude with a reflection on the entire process as a living relationship with Jesus Christ. We center all of our efforts to grow in virtue and to serve others in Jesus. He is the focus, the leitmotif, of all we do.

DISCUSSION QUESTIONS

1. How does the Sacred Heart of Jesus reveal God's love to you?

2. How is our sanctification a response to the love of God?

3. What has the concept of "putting on the heart of Christ" meant for you thus far? What does that practically entail?

THE HUMAN HEART AND ITS LONGING FOR LOVE AND INTERIOR PEACE

"Him whom my soul loves — have you seen him?"
Song of Songs 3:3

WHAT IS THE HEART?
WHAT IS LOVE?

Before any meaningful reflection on the deepest longings of our hearts, we must clarify our understanding of the "heart." What do we even mean when we say "heart?"

We treat things based on what we think they are, and our society frequently reduces love to feelings or inclinations. [5]Listen to most any romantic song and the terms "love" and "feel" are often used interchangeably. "You've Lost That Loving Feeling" by the Righteous Brothers is just one classic example. The problem with such an understanding of the heart and love is that when the loving feeling is gone, so too goes the friendship or marriage: "We've fallen out of love."

To counter such a destructive cultural tendency, Regnum Christi, following the Church's tradition, has always placed a great deal of emphasis on loving primarily with the will. The essence of love is not merely a feeling, but a decision for the good of the other. In other words, love is self-giving: "Not everyone who says to me, 'Lord, Lord,' shall enter the kingdom of heaven, but he who *does* the will of my Father who is in heaven."[6] Your love must translate into action.

This understanding of love avoids the common pitfall of reducing it to a mere sentiment. To love God, spouse, or neighbor requires willpower. The *Ratio Institutionis*, the formation handbook of the Legionaries of Christ, states, "A man without a will is like a leaf or a weather vane, tossed and turned in the wind."[7] In the same vein, Tolkien writes that, "No man, however truly he loved his betrothed and bride as a young man, has lived faithful to her as a wife in mind and body without deliberate conscious exercise of the will, without self-denial."[8] It seems, therefore, that love resides primarily in the will, otherwise your love becomes as dependable as the shifting sands of emotion.

The question then becomes: "Does an emphasis on loving primarily with the will risk ignoring the legitimate role of emotions in loving?" Could we have overcorrected out of fear of sentimentalism? Could it lead to white-knuckling our way through life? Could it lead to an aversion of legitimate expressions of affection?

To answer these questions, let us return to the original question: What is the heart? A good definition goes a long way in avoiding potential pitfalls. Cardinal Ratzinger offered a beautiful and yet clear definition:

❝ In biblical language, the "heart" indicates the center of human life, the point where reason, will, temperament, and sensitivity converge, where the person finds his unity and his interior orientation.[9]

The heart therefore represents the entire interior world of the person. This is much more profound than reducing the heart to mere emotions (or sensitivity), yet it indicates that emotions play a legitimate role in loving.

To say you love someone with all your heart is to say that you love him or her with your entire person. Your intellect seeks to understand the other person better. Your will appreciates the good already in him or her and works tenaciously for that person's continued good.[10] Your emotions, under the guidance of your intellect and reason, enable you to show and receive true and appropriate affection according to your God-given temperament.

This is an integrated understanding of the heart and the human person. We love every facet of the other person—intellect, will, temperament, and sensitivity—with every facet of our own personality. It is integral precisely because all the various elements, each with a particular task, form a harmonious whole.

Now that we have considered what the heart is, let us consider what it desires.

OUR HEART'S LONGINGS FOR LOVE AND PEACE

The human heart, in its entirety, is the seat of our deepest longings. What are those longings? When we speak of a longing, we mean much more than a practical need like hunger and thirst. It is a desire that transcends us and gives us purpose. Some of the basic desires are truth, goodness, beauty, and happiness.[11] For example, our search for truth is not solely for any particular truth, such as $2 + 2 = 4$, but the overarching truth of all of reality: Why is there anything at all instead of nothing? Why are we here, and what must we do?[12] Similarly, we appreciate good things—such as a new car—but are never satisfied with just one good thing for long. Our longing for goodness continues well beyond the lifespan of our car—even a nice one. All these desires are ultimately a reflection of our hunger for God.

Among the existential desires of our heart is love. We long to receive and to give it. However, to love better, we must also possess an interior peace born of order. The greater our peace, the freer we are to love. Therefore, continuing with an integral approach to the human heart, we will consider how our longings to be loved and to give love both benefit from and contribute to an interior peace born of order. Finally, we will consider how all three of these longings–to have interior peace, to be loved, and to love– point to God and prepare us for an encounter with him.

TO BE LOVED

"All You Need is Love" is perhaps one of the most profound truths uttered by the Beatles.[13]

Every faculty of the human person serves a function. The eyes see. Ears hear. The tongue tastes and speaks. Lungs breathe. The intellect thinks. The will desires and decides. The heart, in its entirety, loves. It is in loving that the human person most reveals his grandeur and most perfectly reflects God, in whose image and likeness he is made.[14]

The human person needs to love. However, before we are capable of loving, we must first receive love; that is, we must know that we are lovable. Dr. Conrad Baars is a Catholic psychologist who integrated psychology and spirituality. In his book *Born Only Once*[15] he refers to the need to receive love as being affirmed. In her preface, Dr. Baars's daughter writes that the book, "presents a truth about the human person regarding his or her fundamental psychic need [to receive] affirming love, in order to develop into a mature and happy adult."[16] It seems that the person does not so much learn to love as experience being loved. You learn that you are lovable to the degree that others affirm the goodness they observe in you. This affirmation is a gift that must be received.[17] This is affirmation of who you are, independent of what you do or achieve. You are valued simply for being you.[18] Then, secure in your own goodness, you are able to affirm that goodness in others; that is, you can love them. When a person lacks this initial affirmation, much of life becomes an effort, conscious or unconscious, to prove his or her own worth.[19] Perhaps this understanding clarifies why Our Lord's command to love your neighbor as yourself contains the clause "as yourself."[20] If we are subject to self-loathing or insecurity, we are not capable of maturely loving another person. Baars writes, "It is only after I have received myself first that I can receive the other."[21]

TO LOVE

While our starting point may be to receive love, we also desire to give love.

By its very nature, a loving relationship implies reciprocity. Simply to receive love without seeking to return love would be immature at best. Unrequited love is incomplete. We intuit as much. Our longing for reciprocal love is rooted in our being made in the image and likeness of God, who is Trinity, or a community of total and mutual self-giving.

It is therefore a profound longing of the heart to give love, or, in the words of Viktor Frankl in his book *Man's Search for Meaning*, to live for a mission, something beyond yourself.

*What man actually needs is not a [life without tension] but rather the striving and struggling for a worthwhile goal, a freely chosen task… Everyone has his own specific vocation or mission in life to carry out a concrete assignment which demands fulfillment. Therein he cannot be replaced, nor can his life be repeated.[22]

Frankl even quotes Nietzsche: "He who has a why to live for can bear with almost any how."[23] That is, even the greatest sacrifices can be sustained when shouldered out of love: the countless sleepless nights of parents; the risks of a firefighter, police officer, or soldier; or the ultimate sacrifice of the martyr. It is our mission and our love that motivates us to keep going when things are difficult. This is much more than surviving hardship; it is the secret to thriving as a human being: "unless a grain of wheat falls to the ground and dies, it remains just a grain of wheat; but if it dies, it produces much fruit."[24] As Frankl puts it, "success, like happiness, cannot be pursued; it must ensue, and it only does so as the unintended side-effect of one's dedication to a cause greater than oneself."[25]

INTERIOR PEACE

The human heart also longs for interior peace, yet we often find it missing from our lives. The interior division and turmoil we experience are the fruits of Original Sin and personal sin, our own and that of others: worries, unforgiveness, emotional scars, and insecurities. If we don't deal with it, our interior turmoil will cause turmoil around us. As Thomas à Kempis writes, "First keep peace with yourself; then you will be able to bring peace to others."[26] That is why there is an intimate link between our ability to love and interior peace.

The question becomes, "How do we achieve interior peace?" Referring to the relationship between nations, the Catechism states that peace is "the stability and security of a just order."[27] Analogously, interior peace requires interior order. The disorder introduced by sin must be touched by grace. However, even the grace of baptism, and the subsequent living in a state of grace, does not eliminate our fallen nature's concupiscence.[28] We are still disordered. We are still inclined to sin.

That disorder often plays itself out in the tensions between our emotions and appetites on one side, and our intellect and will on the other. That is, our emotions and other appetites—such as hunger, anger, and the sexual appetite— want to act with little or no guidance from our intellect and will. However, our intellect and our emotions should neither be at war with each other, nor simply coexist side by side with no interaction. They are to act as an integrated whole, each needing the other. The intellect and will must guide the emotions, but the emotions also should enrich and strengthen our reason and willpower. We recognize this reciprocally positive relationship between the emotions, the intellect, and the will in discernment and inspiration.

St. Igantius's discernment of spirits recognizes a particular sentiment present in our heart, and asks, "Why is it there?" An example would be "Why am I upset?" Perhaps we are merely tired, frustrated about not achieving a certain goal, or annoyed that someone was unkind. Once aware of the cause of the emotion, discernment then asks, "What will happen if I follow this emotion? Will it lead to good or evil?"[29] Similarly, discernment seeks to decide, "How should I best respond to this emotion? What would Christ do?" Discernment therefore puts the intellect and will in control, but acknowledges that the emotion is there and relevant. Ignoring our emotions or pushing them away is not only counterproductive (since the unacknowledged emotion will work against our decision to do something), but it could even prove psychologically harmful. Our emotions act like the dashboard on a car indicating that something is happening under the hood. We had better pay attention to those warning lights if we want our car to run well.

Moreover, our intellect and will can also directly benefit from our emotional world. That is, our emotions can inspire us to grasp something much more profoundly than if we approached it by the intellect alone. We call this process "inspiring the heart." Our understanding of something will remain somewhat vague and abstract until our emotions align with a particular truth. That is what we mean when we say that our ideas have to go from our "head" to our "heart." For example, it is one thing to affirm intellectually that God loves you; it is another to experience that love and know it on an emotional level. The emotional experience makes truth more relatable to the individual. It is good to hear "I love you"; it is more concrete to receive a hug. Even the great intellectual, St. Thomas Aquinas, acknowledges this: "Man doesn't know the full truth until his feelings 'know' what his intellect knows."[30]

In the same vein, you only truly get to know something or someone if you love that thing or person first. Our affection for our country, a sport, a type of art or music, a person, or God inclines us to appreciate it, or him or her, more. We want to learn about and discover the good in what we love. In *The Abolition of Man*, C. S. Lewis refers to the Greek and Roman tradition of preparing small children to grasp deeper moral truths by inspiring their imaginations and hearts through story. That is, rather than dryly explaining the importance of bravery, the teacher tells them a story of a soldier nobly sacrificing himself for the good of his country.

This, Lewis says, prepares the way for the children to grasp more abstract concepts later, by cultivating their affection for the good and the beautiful and his rejection of evil. Lewis writes, "Aristotle says that the aim of education is to make the pupil like and dislike what he ought."[31] Holly Ordway, a convert from atheism to Catholicism writes of how grace entered through her imagination.

> Long… before I considered questions of faith and practice, my imagination was being fed Christianity… I had no idea that the *Chronicles of Narnia* had anything to do with Jesus, but images from the stories stuck with me… at some point in my childhood, I found J. R. R. Tolkien's *The Hobbit* and *The Lord of the Rings*, and that changed everything. Not suddenly… But slowly, surely. Like light from an invisible lamp, God's grace was beginning to shine out from Tolkien's works, illuminating my Godless imagination with a Christian vision. …. It was a world in which there is darkness, but also real light, a light that shines in the darkness and is not extinguished: Galadriel's light, and the light of the star that Sam sees break through the clouds in Mordor… The Lord of the Rings was where I first encountered the evangelium, the good news. I didn't know, then, that my imagination had been, as it were, baptized in Middle-earth.[32]

This is why books such as Lewis's *Chronicles of Narnia* and Tolkien's *Lord of the Rings* are so important in forming a profoundly Christian worldview for children and adults.

INTERIOR PEACE AND LOVE ARE MUTUALLY BENEFICIAL

When we achieve a certain harmony between our emotions, intellect, and will, each playing its proper role in relation to the others, there is greater peace. As we have seen, while interior peace is to some degree its own goal, it is also a means that enables the person to love God and others with greater freedom.[33] When we possess peace that is what we will communicate.

Reciprocally, loving others brings greater peace, because it is in loving others that we take our gaze off ourselves. Our selfishness and sin rob us of peace; a healthy self-forgetfulness restores it. That said, interior order is oriented toward and subordinate to love, since love, expressed in the fulfillment of our mission, is the ultimate goal of all our formation and efforts.[34]

ALL OUR DESIRES POINT TO GOD AND PREPARE US TO ENCOUNTER HIM

These three desires—to be loved, to love, and to have interior peace—can be lived on a natural level. We can love and be loved by our family. We can obtain a certain interior peace and order through the exercise of self-control. Nevertheless, all of these desires ultimately point to our desire for God. When we love and when we are loved, there is contentment, but there is also a desire for more, and in that "more" we find God. Our unlimited desire for love points to the need for a love without limits that only God can give. Therefore, the deepest longings of our heart are ultimately a longing for God. As St. Augustine writes, "You made us for yourself, and our heart is restless, until it rests in you."[35] Our heart is longing, and the heart of Jesus is the reply.

"Him whom my soul loves — have you seen him?"
Song of Songs 3:3

DISCUSSION QUESTIONS

1. Generally, have you considered the heart in merely emotional terms, or with an integral understanding? Is such a distinction new to you?

2. What are some potential consequences of either reducing love to a mere emotion or ignoring emotion all together?

3. What are some of the more evident longings of your heart?

4. In contemplating your deepest longings, what place does being loved, showing love, and interior peace have?

5. Which interior longing has most impelled you to look for God?

ATTRIBUTES OF JESUS'S HEART

"...when I found him whom my soul loves."
Song of Songs 3:4

THE HEART THAT LOVES US AND FILLS OUR DEEPEST LONGINGS

The longings of the heart to be loved, to love, and to have interior peace are most perfectly fulfilled in our relationship with the heart of Jesus.

Jesus profoundly fills our desire to be loved. The very essence of the Gospel or the "Good News" is that God loved us so much that he died and rose for us, so that we could have eternal life: "For God so loved the world that he gave his only Son, so that everyone who believes in him might not perish but might have eternal life."[36] It is a personal love that God has for each one of us.

❝The Son of God... loved me and gave himself for me.' He has loved us all with a human heart. For this reason, the Sacred Heart of Jesus, pierced by our sins and for our salvation, 'is quite rightly considered the chief sign and symbol of that... love with which the divine Redeemer continually loves the eternal Father and all human beings' without exception.[37]

Those who have received little human love may finally experience it in Christ. Those blessed to have received human love still long for the perfection of love that only Christ can give. His love affirms us and accepts us for who we are "without exception."

Even when Christ calls out our sinfulness and challenges us, it is always for our well-being and conversion. That is why St. Paul affirms, "God proves his love for us in that while we were still sinners Christ died for us."[38]

Therefore, meeting Christ, as our creator and redeemer necessarily affirms our goodness as his creatures and as redeemed sinners. In "Night's Bright Darkness," Sally Read comments on her conversion, "No one argued me down from any of my 'liberal' or 'progressive' positions, but the logic of Christ's love was penetrating deeper and deeper into my heart. I was aware of being known as I never had been before."[39] We encounter unconditional love from Jesus, and that experience changes us.

Our desire to love others greatly increases through our experience of Jesus's love for us. Then, in loving others for his sake, we experience profound joy. St. Patrick recounts in his *Confession*:

> [Having returned to Britain after being a slave in Ireland] I saw in a vision of the night a man... coming as it were from Ireland with countless letters. He gave me one of them... which was entitled, 'The Voice of the Irish.' And whilst I was reading aloud... I heard the voices of those who... cried... 'We beseech thee, holy youth, to come and walk once more amongst us.' And I was exceedingly touched in my heart... and so I awoke. Thanks be to God, after many years the Lord granted [my return] according to their earnest cry.[40]

This vision moved St. Patrick's heart; it filled him with joy, and the Church is still benefiting from the fruits of that joy today. Like St. Patrick, we all long to discover and follow the mission for which we were created.

The love of Jesus brings us interior peace. It is a peace "that surpasses all understanding [and] will guard your hearts and minds in Christ Jesus."[41] This peace normally comes through baptism, which purifies us from our sins and brings about a new birth in the Holy Spirit,[42] or through confession, which allows the recovery of lost grace.[43] However, God's grace and peace is not limited to the sacraments. He may reach a soul at any moment to draw him or her closer to himself and the Church. This peace is a work of grace but also a fruit of an encounter with our Savior. He begins to place order in a person's life where there was none. His or her interior begins to mend. Jesus's continued presence sustains that peace; although it is a peace where we must still struggle to master ourselves (as we will see later). In her autobiographical conversion story, *Something Other Than God*, Jennifer Fulwiler comments on her conversation with a kind and devout Catholic woman:

As she spoke, it reminded me of what I'd read of the lives of the saints. For as diverse a group of folks as the saints were, the one thing they had in common is that the people around them always remarked on their peace. To know a saint, I'd heard, was to know someone who was so in tune with God that he became a channel of supernatural love. Not necessarily through his way with words or his great deeds, but through mere presence, infused by something not of this earth. I'd always wondered what it would be like to meet someone like that. And now I was pretty sure I knew.[44]

This peace of the saints goes hand in hand with the joy of loving others by sharing the Gospel, because what you are actually sharing is the very peace you possess: Jesus Christ.

FIVE ATTRIBUTES OF THE HEART OF JESUS

When we love there is a growing desire to contemplate the beloved. Then as our contemplation makes us more aware of the other's goodness, our love grows. If this is the case in human love, it is all the more so with our love for Christ, the perfect man. Archbishop Goodier writes:

*There has lived in this world one man in whom, if he is taken wholly, no fault whatsoever has been found, who has shown himself in all things perfect, whose accurate picture, moreover, has been handed down for us all to study... not only by followers who love his name... but by unbelievers also, who would look on him with cold eyes, unenthusiastic in his cause... and yet would be honest and sincere. They have scrutinized Jesus, the Carpenter of Nazareth, and have found him to be 'the Lamb of God,' 'the King of Israel.' They have listened to and sifted his words, and have acknowledged that 'never did man speak as this man spoke.' They have weighed all his deeds and have declared that 'he hath done all things well.'... They have looked for a charge against him and have owned with Pilate, 'I find no fault in this just man.' They have pierced his heart, and what they have found there has made them confess: "Indeed this was the Son of God."[45]

Therefore, motivated by love and with a desire to grow in that love, marveling at the perfection we believe by faith and have already experienced in our own prayer and our own lives, let us look more closely at the heart of Jesus.

Since Jesus is the perfect man and contains all the human virtues,[46] it is hard to choose which ones to consider. However, since this essay is reflecting specifically upon the harmony of an ordered interior, we will focus on five pertinent attributes: equanimity, emotional richness, affection, self-assuredness, and passion.

EQUANIMITY

Try to find a moment when Christ was not in control of his reactions. He always showed an "evenness of mind especially under stress."[47]

Jesus was patient with the crowd: healing countless people, feeding them, and casting out demons.[48] When we recall that the crowd was so insistent that Jesus and his disciples barely had time to eat or rest, Our Lord's patience is all the more impressive.[49] At least once Jesus had to preach from a boat to avoid being crushed by the crowd.[50]

Jesus was gentle but also willing to challenge his apostles: explaining parables, defending them from the attack of the Pharisees, correcting John and James for wanting to call down fire on a village, and calling Peter "Satan" because he was not thinking as God does.[51]

Jesus could show anger, but always in a measured way, with self-control. He called the Pharisees and Scribes a "brood of vipers," and he drove the traders and animals out of the Temple with a cord.[52] Nevertheless, his equanimity is all the more remarkable when you consider that Christ's enemies were relentless in their opposition to them. As Bishop Goodier points out, "if we would gauge the character of Jesus aright we must never lose sight of [the Pharisees' and Scribes'] constant, determined, [and] merciless hatred which from first to last hung about him, sparing no pains to counteract every good word he said, to thwart every good deed he did."[53]

Jesus showed fear but remained determined in the face of danger, especially in Gethsemane and during his Passion.[54] He was afraid to the point of sweating blood but still could tell the Father, "not my will but yours be done."[55] Clearly, our Lord's divinity did not spare his humanity the natural fear of suffering and death. To overcome the fear, he needed the strengthening of grace and the virtue of equanimity.

G. K. Chesterton, in his work Orthodoxy, points out that Christian equanimity is not mediocrity, simply refraining from doing or having too much of something. It is not the equivalent to the Roman motto "virtue is found in the middle."[56] Rather, it is balancing two "competing" virtues and living both. Chesterton gives the example of St. Joan of Arc. In her, you have the simplicity of a country girl and the boldness of a warrior, both lived in full force.[57]

This balance between competing virtues observed in Christ has always been an essential part of the Regnum Christi spirituality. For example, members are called to be contemplative and evangelizing; humble and apostolic leaders; unique individuals and team players.[58] Similarly, Goodier writes that Jesus is the "strongest of men yet treated as the weakest; the most commanding yet the most submissive; the most severe yet the most considerate; the most friendly yet the most exclusive... the paradox, in him, implies no contradiction, it is essential to his portrait."[59] In Jesus, this paradox was harmonious; it touched upon his very being, fully God and fully man.[60]

EMOTIONAL RICHNESS

Jesus was comfortable having, acknowledging, and showing his feelings. He had a rich emotional world.

He was surprised that his parents did not think to find him in the Temple.[61] He became angered and grieved at the Pharisees' hardness of heart.[62] He was astonished at the Centurion's faith.[63] He rejoiced in the faith of the little ones.[64] He had pity on the crowd that was like sheep without a shepherd.[65] He chastised the towns that showed little faith after witnessing many of his miracles.[66] He felt indignation when the apostles tried to keep the children from him.[67] He marveled at the widow's generosity in the Temple treasury.[68] He showed frustration when the apostles could not cast out the demon causing a young man's convulsions.[69] He wept with Martha and Mary near the tomb of Lazarus.[70] He expressed gratitude to Mary for anointing him before his passion.[71] He was afraid in Gethsemane.[72] He showed disappointment in Judas.[73] He revealed his sense of abandonment both in Gethsemane and on the cross.[74] He reveled in victory on the cross with a loud cry, "It is accomplished."[75]

Jesus showed us that our gamut of emotions is part of our human reality. If ever we were tempted to an emotionless stoicism, we need only contemplate Christ to allow ourselves to have and share a wide variety of feelings. It was precisely Jesus's equanimity or self-control that gave him the freedom to be at peace with his emotional world. We can only marvel at the integral harmony found in Our Lord.

AFFECTION

Affection is not seeking a desired emotion for oneself; rather, it is oriented toward the other, showing them "fondness or tenderness."

Affection is related to charity, with the added component of showing a certain tenderness with the action. It is putting your emotional world at the service of others, regardless of how you may feel interiorly at a given moment. Think of the mother whose baby has been crying for most of the day. The mother feels tired and probably cranky, and yet she shows tenderness to her child—smiling, embracing, and even singing to him or her. She is being truly affectionate, and not merely pretending to be. To be consistently affectionate towards others requires great self-control, charity, and abnegation.

The five love languages, based on the book by Gary Chapman, can prove useful in categorizing some of the different ways in which Our Lord shows countless signs of affection. They are words of affirmation, acts of service, gifts, quality time, and touch.[76]

Jesus used words of affirmation. Before referencing her sinful cohabitation, he first told the Samaritan woman that she had answered correctly about not being married.[77] When the scribe responded wisely, Jesus said, "You are not far from the kingdom of God."[78] Commenting on the centurion he said, "I have not seen such faith in all Israel."[79] Walking on water, he assured the terrified apostles, "It is I. Do not be afraid."[80] At the house of Simon the Pharisee, Jesus comments that the sinful woman was forgiven, because "she has shown great love."[81] Upon return from their mission, Jesus told the seventy-two disciples to "rejoice because your names are written in heaven."[82] While gently correcting Martha's worry, he affirmed Mary's contemplation as having "chosen the better part."[83] To the repentant thief on the cross, Jesus said that "today you will be with me in Paradise."[84]

Jesus constantly performed acts of service. He fed the hungry, such as the five thousand with only two fish and five loaves.[85] He cured countless sick throughout Galilee, the Decapolis, and Judea.[86] He cast out demons, like those tormenting the man from Gerasenes who he sent into the swine.[87] He taught the ignorant, like his disciples at the Sermon on the Mount.[88] He encouraged the brokenhearted, such as Jairus before the miracle.[89] He forgave sinners, like the paralytic lowered through the roof.[90]

Jesus gave his followers countless gifts, particularly from Holy Thursday to Pentecost. At the Last Supper he gave us the gift of the priesthood and the Eucharist.[91] At the foot of the cross he gave us Mary to be our mother.[92] On the cross he gave us his very heart, pouring out blood and water, which revealed his mercy and gave birth to the Church[93]. After the Resurrection, he gave the apostles the power to forgive sins.[94] At Pentecost he gave the Church the gift of the Holy Spirit, who leads us in all truth.[95]

Jesus spent quality time with people. He lived with Mary and Joseph for the entirety of his hidden life, mostly in Nazareth.[96] He spent three days with the teachers in the Temple, asking and answering questions.[97] He met with Nicodemus for a private audience at night.[98] He pushed himself, and his apostles, to fatigue to arrive in time to meet the Samaritan woman at the well in Sychar and then spent two days with the entire town.[99] He dined with Matthew and other tax collectors and sinners.[100] He also dined with Zacchaeus, Simon the Leper, and Lazarus.[101] Jesus often took the apostles away from the crowds to rest and to learn from him.[102]

Jesus would show affection through touch. When healing others, he frequently did so by touching them, such as with the leper,[103] the deaf man in whose ear he put his finger,[104] and the blind man in whose eyes he smeared clay.[105] He placed his hands on the children to bless them.[106] He took Jairus's daughter by the hand when restoring her to life.[107] Once risen, Our Lord encouraged Thomas to put his finger in his hands and side.[108]

Jesus went about doing good.[109] In both word and deed he revealed the love and tenderness of the Father. That is why the Gospel of John could characterize Jesus's mission as showing that "God so loved the world that he gave his only Son."[110] This affection and tenderness give us poor sinners the confidence to approach Our Lord for forgiveness and grace. Msgr. Bougaud states it beautifully,

Had Jesus not done a single miracle, the world still would have prostrated itself at his feet; inversely, had he worked thousands of more miracles, more incredible ones, if he had not added to such works moral beauty, sweetness, discretion, and infinite tenderness, rather than attract others to himself, he would have scared and repelled them. In the mind of the ancients… supernatural power was not inevitably linked to the ideas of God and goodness. They look at it as something proper to bad spirits as well as good ones, and [that power] frequently inspired terror as much as respect.[111]

SELF-ASSUREDNESS

Jesus was self-assured, confident. He was comfortable in his own skin. In him, there was a complete absence of insecurity. This was not arrogance. There was no pride in him, which is why he could say, "I am meek and humble of heart."[112] If equanimity brings peace through self-control, self-assuredness brings peace through a clear sense of identity.[113]

Our Lord's self-assuredness enabled him to interact with all types of people without a shadow of awkwardness or insecurity on his part. He dealt with his disciples, women, Pharisees, Scribes, Roman soldiers, Samaritans, foreigners, tax collectors, prostitutes, the poor, the sick, the possessed, farmers, and fishermen. He was able to adjust his speech and illustrations to the level of his interlocutor. He spoke of the law to Nicodemus, of planting to farmers, and of kingdoms to Pilate.[114]

Since Jesus had no need to affirm his ego, he was free to serve others. People often perceive when someone seeks their good without ulterior motives. They gravitate toward such people. This was very much the case with Jesus. Simple souls were irresistibly drawn to him. Recognizing that same quality in St. John XXIII, Dr. Baars writes,

> Many of my patients… told me during the years that John was Pontiff that they were always deeply moved when they watched him on television. [Pope John] made them feel good and happy with themselves… They 'knew'… that they were important to John, that he loved them as they were, that they experienced the effect of affirmation.

People who had met John in person used to remark that in his presence they did not feel themselves being judged, but loved for what they were.[115]

If affection is an action that draws people to a person, then self-assurance is a way of being that also draws. If St. John XXIII had such a powerful effect on people, imagine Our Lord's capacity to do the same.

PASSION

Christ's heart was full of passion. If affection is the tenderness associated with one's actions, passion is the intensity with which the action is done.

We often falsely equate someone with self-control as lacking passion: "He's a rather passionless guy." While there is a tension, there is no contradiction between being passionate and exercising self-control. This balance is preeminently the case with Jesus.

There were distinct moments when Christ's passionate love for his Father and souls particularly revealed itself. He confronted Satan in the desert and firmly rejected his temptations with "Get away, Satan! It is written: 'The Lord, your God, shall you worship and him alone shall you serve.'"[116] After driving the traders and money changers out of the temple, his apostles recalled the Scripture which said, "Zeal for your house will consume me."[117] He confronted the Pharisees with anger and grief by healing the man with the withered hand on the Sabbath.[118] Yet in these, as in all moments, Jesus remained fully self-possessed.

Ultimately, everything Jesus did he did fully, with every fiber of his being. This was true of his prayer: frequently getting up early in the morning, as when he decided to move on from Capernaum;[119] at other times praying all night long, as he did before calling the Twelve to himself;[120] and even praying to the point of sweating blood in Gethsemane.[121] He lived his ministry with intensity: not finding time to eat[122] and being so exhausted that he slept through a storm on a boat.[123]

It was, however, his passion and death where Jesus most revealed the intensity of his love. At the Last Supper he clearly stated that he would freely suffer because "the world must know that I love the Father and that I do just as the Father has commanded me."[124] During his passion, Jesus quite literally gave his all, to the last drop of blood as the lance pierced his heart.[125]

This is the same Jesus that said in Revelation, "because you are lukewarm, neither hot nor cold, I will spit you out of my mouth."[126] Therefore, the invitation is clear; he calls us to love with an equal intensity of love. This intensity is not altered by temperament [which only changes how the intensity is lived], but by the conviction of faith. Having encountered Jesus's intense love for us, we should wish to respond with an equal intensity, or at least with as much intensity as we can.

THE TWO LOVES WHICH UNIFY ALL OF JESUS'S ENDEAVORS

The five characteristics just considered were present in the heart of Jesus. These characteristics, and all the others, were not the object of his attention but expressions of it. He was not constantly thinking about "being virtuous"; rather, he possessed in his heart two primary loves which drove all his actions. These two loves were the focus for which he exercised all his virtues and energy. These two loves are his Father and humanity.

Jesus's first love was the Father. He made constant reference to his Father: "Why were you looking for me? Did you not know that I must be in my Father's house?"[127] "The Father and I are one."[128] "Everyone who acknowledges me before others I will acknowledge before my heavenly Father."[129] "No one knows the Son except the Father, and no one knows the Father except the Son."[130] When making decisions he references the will of the Father: "Let us go on to the nearby villages that I may preach there also. For this purpose have I come."[131] When discouraged, he seeks to draw strength by remembering these two loves, "I am troubled now. Yet what should I say? 'Father, save me from this hour'? But it was for this purpose that I came to this hour. Father, glorify your name."[132]

Jesus's second love was for others. It was a consequence of his love for the Father, who sent him to reunite fallen man with his Father: "For God so loved the world that he gave his only Son, so that everyone who believes in him might not perish but might have eternal life."[133] He is the shepherd who goes "after the lost one until he finds it… And when he does find it, he sets it on his shoulders with great joy."[134]

During his greatest suffering, Jesus kept these two loves, the Father and others, at the forefront of his mind. In Gethsemane he prayed, "My Father, if it is not possible that this cup pass without my drinking it, your will be done!"[135] Hanging on the cross, he cried out, "My God, my God, why have you forsaken me?"[136] He was quoting

Psalm 22, which is a prayer confiding in God amidst suffering, and the promise he gives to souls:

> For he has not spurned or disdained the misery of this poor wretch, Did not turn away from me, but heard me when I cried out. I will offer praise in the great assembly; my vows I will fulfill before those who fear him. The poor will eat their fill; those who seek the LORD will offer praise. May your hearts enjoy life forever! All the ends of the earth will remember and turn to the LORD; All the families of nations will bow low before him[137].

Jesus experienced wretchedness on the cross but knew he was not disdained by the Father. He sacrificed himself so that others may enjoy life forever in heaven. Even Jesus's last two words from the cross point to these two loves. He declared his salvific mission complete: "It is finished."[138] Finally, he stated, "Father, into your hands I commend my spirit,"[139] and expired.

His love for the Father and humanity was the context for all the attributes of his heart. He lived and died for these two loves.

JESUS AS MODEL OF THE INTEGRAL HEART

Taken together, the five attributes we have briefly reflected upon—equanimity, emotional richness, affection, self-assuredness, and passion—show the integrity and order within the heart of Jesus. Each faculty—intellect, will, emotions, and appetites—played its proper role in harmony with the others. Jesus's intellect and will channeled his emotions and appetites to the fulfillment of his mission, which is the salvation of souls for the glory of his Father. Only in the context of this self-forgetting love, do the virtues make sense, or even remain virtues.

This interior harmony of Jesus's human heart enabled his divinity to shine through more perfectly: "Whoever has seen me has seen the Father."[140] Similarly, as disciples of Jesus, we are called to work towards an ever more integrally formed heart so that his grace and message may shine more perfectly through us. This is the purpose of Regnum Christi's integral formation, our next consideration.

"...when I found him whom my soul loves."
Song of Songs 3:4

DISCUSSION QUESTIONS

1. When and how did you first consciously experience Jesus's love for you?

2. What attributes of the heart of Jesus do you find most attractive? What do you most admire about him?

3. Have you noticed and admired the equanimity in the person of Jesus? Which Gospel passage has best reflected this quality to you?

4. How does Jesus's ability to have and express a gamut of emotions affect you?

PUTTING ON THE HEART OF JESUS

"I held him and would not let him go..." Song of Songs 3:4

How do we hold onto Jesus and not let him go? It is perhaps more precise to say that he is the one who holds onto us. How then do we remain in his embrace? Regnum Christi responds through integral formation, which is an ongoing process of becoming always like Christ in every facet of our personality. We seek to put on the heart of Jesus.

This section will attempt neither to enumerate nor to explain all the facets of formation in Regnum Christi (usually divided into four categories: spiritual, human, intellectual, and apostolic). Rather, it will highlight three principles to keep in mind while working on the formation of our heart, particularly when we seek to grow in virtue through repetition. Those three principles are reliance upon grace, collaboration with grace through our own effort, and perseverance in our efforts. While these principles apply to all areas of formation, they are also useful in the formation of our heart: achieving an ordered interior, and learning to love ever more like Christ by imitating the attributes of his heart.

RELIANCE UPON GRACE

"I am the vine, you are the branches. Whoever remains in me and I in him will bear much fruit, because without me you can do nothing."[141] We have received our very existence from God. He is our Creator.[142] Similarly, our supernatural life is a gift from God. "Grace is favor, the free and undeserved help that God gives us to respond to his call to become children of God."[143] In relation to God, we are in many ways like infants who are fully reliant on their parents. This explains the crucial importance of the sacraments, which are Christ's actions in our souls: introducing us to the life of grace through baptism; the recuperation of lost grace through confession; and the increasing of grace through the Eucharist.[144]

Therefore, in our effort to be both saints and apostles—our two-fold baptismal vocation—we must rely fully on God's grace. A common temptation among devout souls is to desire sanctity or to achieve some apostolic goal by relying solely on our own efforts. We may not intentionally push him away, but we can often compartmentalize things to such a degree that we forget to turn to Jesus. This well-intentioned self-reliance frequently gets us into trouble.

St. Peter seemed to have the same difficulty on the evening of the Last Supper: "'Lord, I am prepared to go to prison and to die with you.' But [Jesus] replied, 'I tell you, Peter, before the cock crows this day, you will deny three times that you know me.'"[145] Peter's love for Jesus was sincere; it was real. He had left everything to follow Jesus. He even tried to defend Jesus with the sword in Gethsemane. However, when things no longer went according to plan, Peter lost heart to the point of denying Our Lord three times. Peter relied too much on his own strength in his effort to be faithful to Jesus and his strength was found lacking.

As a remedy, we must develop the habit of turning to God as a first response to any given situation: "Lord, what would you have me do?" "Lord, please help." He is our reference point. He is our strength. We place our confidence in him. We ask him to make our efforts fruitful.

This reliance on God's grace is a crucial antidote to pride or discouragement. When we think we have nothing else to give, we remember that Jesus's strength sustains us. St. John Chrysostom's homily before going into exile beautifully depicts such confidence:

> Am I in good heart by my own strength? I hold his written word. This is my staff, this is my courage, this is to me a calm harbor. Even if the world be troubled, I hold that written word; I look up to those words, they are a wall of strength to me. What are they? 'I am with you always until the consummation of the world.' Christ is with me, what shall I fear? If waves are raging against me, and the fountains of the deep and the passions of princes, all these things are more insignificant than a cobweb. And if it were not for your charity, I would not refuse to depart tomorrow, for I always say, Lord, may Thy will be done; not what this man or that man wishes, but as Thou wilt. This is my tower of defense, this is my immutable rock, this is my sure staff. If this be God's will, so be it. If he wish me to remain here, I am grateful to him. Wherever it may be, I give him thanks.[146]

COLLABORATION WITH GRACE

We must also collaborate with God's grace through our efforts. While it is true that the apostles had to rely on Jesus in the feeding of the five thousand men, not counting women and children,[147] it is equally true that in that same miracle Jesus asked the apostles to bring him the loaves and fish and then to distribute them. He could have rained manna from heaven, or simply made the food appear in the hands of the people.[148] Our Lord clearly wanted the apostles to learn that without him they could do nothing. However, he also wanted them to learn that he desired to work miracles through them. Jesus desired their collaboration, and he desires ours.

There is no inherent conflict between our reliance upon grace and our work. When we are responsive to grace, God moves us to action. That is why St. James can write, "Indeed someone may say, 'You have faith and I have works.' Demonstrate your faith to me without works, and I will demonstrate my faith to you from my works."[149] God does not ask us to be passive or lacking in effort. Rather, he asks us to be docile, that is, dependent on his grace and his direction in all that we do. A good racehorse is perfectly docile to the jockey even while running at full speed.

As such, our free response to the grace of Our Lord, both in our sanctification and apostolate, requires constant effort. Specific to our efforts to become more Christlike, Regnum Christi encourages the use of a program of life, which is simply a game plan to work intentionally on a given virtue. First, we identify our root sin, the area in which we most struggle (whether pride, vanity, or sensuality), and then we choose the contrary virtue in which we want to grow. If pride is our struggle, humility would be the virtue in which we should grow. We do so by practicing it many times a day. On some days we may listen more attentively; on others we may show more gratitude; still on others we may acquiesce on nonessentials out of charity—all with the desire to practice humility. This focus on a particular virtue will help us both to grow and to avoid the common temptation of frequently changing our game plan.

PERSEVERANCE

Becoming more like Jesus takes time. Learning to rely more on grace and live by virtue requires practice. Consequently, patient perseverance is of the essence in our Christian journey.

Often our frustrations in the spiritual and apostolic life boil down to impatience. We get angry and frustrated that we are not yet as holy or as apostolically fruitful as we would like. Sanctity is not the decision of one day; it is the task of a lifetime. St. Paul, with his intensely passionate and blunt personality, must have fought many battles of self-conquest before he could authentically give witness to the fact that:

❝Love is patient, love is kind. It is not jealous, [love] is not pompous, it is not inflated, it is not rude, it does not seek its own interests, it is not quick-tempered, it does not brood over injury, it does not rejoice over wrongdoing but rejoices with the truth. It bears all things, believes all things, hopes all things, endures all things.[150]

We should be neither frightened nor disheartened when we still struggle in our endeavor to be more like Jesus. Rather than discourage us, our shortcomings should help to keep us humble, be more empathetic with the weaknesses of others, rely more on God's grace, and grow in our desire to love more. We must accept the fact that we will struggle in this life. We should run as if in a marathon, not a sprint. Our Lord will provide us with the graces needed for each moment.[151]

There is no perseverance without the cross. Whoever "does not take up his cross and follow after me is not worthy of me."[152] On one hand, the cross consists in the natural sacrifices that the fulfillment of our duties and our effort to grow in virtue entail. Even our secular society understands this. "'No pain, no gain' is an American modern mini-narrative… [which holds] that the road to achievement runs only through hardship."[153] On the other hand, the Christian understands that uniting our effort to the cross of Jesus gives it a salvific value. This especially happens in the celebration of the Eucharist, where "the sacrifice of Christ becomes also the sacrifice of the members of his Body… [in which] their praise, sufferings, prayer, and work, are united with those of Christ and with his total offering, and so acquire a new value."[154] Understanding such value is why St. Paul can write, "But may I never boast except in the cross of our Lord Jesus Christ, through which the world has been crucified to me, and I to the world."[155] St. Paul's boast is not born of morbidity; rather it was a deep understanding that when we carry the cross with Jesus there is great joy. That is why he could also write, "Rejoice in the Lord always. I shall say it again: rejoice!"[156]

To conclude this section, in our endeavor to imitate the virtues found in the heart of Jesus, it is important to rely upon God's grace, collaborate with that grace, and persevere in our efforts. Our goal is heaven. The journey will be arduous and require us to carry our cross, but that journey will be sweet if we keep our eyes focused upon Jesus along the way. That will be the theme of our next, and final, section.

"I held him and would not let him go..."
Song of Songs 3:4

DISCUSSION QUESTIONS

1. How aware are you of the importance of grace? How do you practically rely on God's grace? Are there times you forget to do so? How can you daily remind yourself to rely on grace?

2. How should your own efforts and grace interact? What does that look like practically? Think of an example.

3. What motivates you to persevere when things become difficult? How willing are you to embrace the cross?

CONCLUSION:
RELATIONSHIP WITH JESUS

Benjamin Franklin was quite the achiever. While raised a Puritan, Franklin later rejected Christian doctrine, and described himself as a Deist, albeit one who believed in Providence and the value of prayer. He always retained an appreciation for the practice of virtue in personal and public life.[157] His striving to grow personally bore abundant fruit: "Despite being born into a poor family and only receiving two years of formal schooling, Franklin became a successful printer, scientist, musician, and author… and in his spare time he helped found a country, and then serve as its diplomat."[158] One of his pursuits was to achieve moral perfection. To do so, he made a list of thirteen virtues and tracked his performance. After some time he observed, "Tho' I never arrived at the perfection I had been so ambitious of obtaining, but fell far short of it, yet I was, by the endeavor, a better and a happier man than I otherwise should have been if I had not attempted it." [159]

We must commend Benjamin Franklin for his pursuit of virtue. The Church has always acknowledged the goodness of human virtue wherever found. Nevertheless, we must draw a crucial distinction between his project and the program of life as lived in the Regnum Christi Movement. The difference is not in the practical application; both approaches identify a virtue, practice it daily, and examine the results. The difference lies in relationship.

The Regnum Christi member seeks to center his or her entire life in Christ. The Statutes state:

❝Our spirituality is centered above all on Jesus Christ and born from experiencing his love. We seek to respond to our Friend and Lord with a personal, real, passionate, and faithful love. Through the action of the Holy Spirit, we are sons and daughters in the Son who becomes the center, standard, and model of our life. We learn to encounter him in the Gospel, the Eucharist, the cross, and our neighbor.[160]

All our efforts at formation are within the context of our relationship with Jesus, and the focus is on the formation of our hearts, the entire heart, "where reason, will, temperament, and sensitivity converge."[161] Therefore, Regnum Christi members "seek to clothe ourselves with Christ in our hearts and in our works," and "let ourselves be permeated by Christ's love for humanity."[162]

Consequently, if the center of our relationship with Jesus is to "put on the heart of Jesus," then we must consider the longings of our hearts, the heart of Jesus, and the means to become more like him. That has been the intent of this essay. It also hopes to encourage that contemplation and imitation.

May we never lose sight of the sanctity and beauty of the heart of Jesus. God willing, we will spend a lifetime and an eternity contemplating that beauty. Our contemplation is not the philosopher's consideration of an abstract idea but the loving gaze between Our Savior and each one of us. May that gaze bring us to reflect him more perfectly and share him with an ever-growing passion.

We entrust our desire to our mother, the Blessed Virgin Mary.

DISCUSSION QUESTIONS

1. How can you best center your efforts for personal sanctification and apostolate on your relationship with Jesus?

2. What helps you to better contemplate the heart of Jesus?

3. What practical resolution will you make as fruit of this study of the heart of Jesus?

EPILOGUE:
WHO IS JESUS FOR ME?

At least two people whom I respect have told me that in writing about Jesus, I should share my own relationship with Jesus with the reader. Paraphrasing the words of St. Paul VI, I must witness if I hope to teach.[163] Therefore, I've decided to write a few lines about my own relationship with Jesus in this epilogue. If the main text was about that which is admirable in Jesus per se, this epilogue will seek to answer the question, "Who is Jesus for me?"

BACKSTORY

I was raised Catholic, but faith at home consisted primarily in Sunday Mass and saying prayers just before bedtime—that was about it. Then, when I was about eleven years old, my mom had a conversion by giving her life to God through praying the Catholic version of a prayer of surrender. She changed immediately.

She began to pray constantly, not locked away in a room or a chapel, but amidst all the tasks of daily life: laundry, cooking, shopping. She would constantly ask Jesus for help, and he seemed to answer. There was joy and excitement. She was in love.

As an only child, this naturally intrigued me. It was fascinating to see the change, and I was still too young to protest or be skeptical. Nevertheless, even at that age I intuitively realized that I had to make my own journey. I had to encounter God. However, until I witnessed the change in my mom, I didn't even know something was missing. Faith meant "saying prayers." I now saw in my mom that it meant a relationship with God, which changes everything.

For example, one afternoon my mom was about to open a pickle jar and thought to herself, "Surely I don't need God's help to open a jar; I can do that myself." But she couldn't open it, so she asked me to help. "You hold; I'll twist." No luck. "I'll hold; you twist." No luck. "Let's grab it with the towel." No luck. "Let's try hot water." No luck. "Bang it on the counter." No luck. Even the jar wrench did not work. After about ten minutes of effort, we were out of breath for trying. She turned to me and said, "Maybe we should say a prayer." So, we began, "Hail Mary… Amen." Immediately and effortlessly, the jar opened. No, it was not the parting of the Red Sea, but it was a key moment in my faith journey. I realized that God is real, that God answers prayers, even mine, even with things as insignificant as opening a jar. God cares about me. He notices.

Early on, the Blessed Mother became an integral part of my faith journey. When I was still eleven, a pilgrim statue of the Blessed Mother came to our parish. Mom invited me to pray the Rosary to ask Mary for help with something that had been bothering me. We went. The prayer was answered. I was excited. Mom asked, "Do you want to pray the Rosary daily?" I said, "yes," and so we did. I wasn't always fervent, or focused, or even awake, but we did pray it daily. If I did fall asleep, Mom would wake me, often using a couch pillow as a preferred projectile. About a month into praying the Rosary, the idea of the priesthood was quietly, but clearly, present in my mind and heart.

After finishing my university studies and working for a couple of years, I entered the novitiate of the Legionaries of Christ. I was ordained a priest in 2002. I lived and worked in California for ten years doing youth work and college chaplaincy. I currently work in

Cincinnati, Ohio, as a retreat director and spiritual guide for the Regnum Christi Movement, and as part-time chaplain at Northern Kentucky University.

WHO IS JESUS FOR ME?

Jesus is a faithful friend. As do all families, ours went through some difficult times. During that time, I was distinctly aware that Jesus was always there helping us. He did not spare us from the difficulties; rather he protected us from what could have been a lot worse. He stayed close to us through thick and thin. He has drawn many graces from those difficulties, including, my own vocation. Jesus has been faithful to me during my life in the Legion. His smile, his humor, and his determination were my strength when I had little of my own.

I have heard his voice speak to my heart, or simply been aware of his presence.

Jesus is attentive to details. I have often noticed his little gifts of kindness that might seem like a coincidence were it not for the perspective of faith. His timing is exquisite. Once, when I was particularly down, someone came up to me and gave me a hug. Another time while I was riding my bike, he showed me several beautiful birds and some deer. I asked him to show me a buck, a rare sight, and he did.

He has called me to battle for him and his kingdom in his Legion. I am honored to carry the initials "LC" at the end of my name. He has given me many Godly brothers in the Legion, and many Godly brothers and sisters in Regnum Christi, both consecrated and lay.

Jesus has inserted me into his ministry of saving souls. On several occasions, he has touched others through me, either through preaching, in spiritual direction, or in the confessional. I have said "just the right thing," without a possibility of naturally knowing what that would be. I have the privilege of having a front seat in his work of grace in souls. He has let me know that I am stepping on sacred ground. He also asks me to intercede for souls.

He comes into my hands daily in the celebration of the Mass. "Who am I that my Lord should come to me?"

He is present in the Tabernacle. There he patiently waits for me. There he gives me peace and strength. He also has broad shoulders upon which I may cry. As a religious, I have the singular grace of having a chapel in my home. I try to spend a fair amount of time with him daily in the chapel.

His love for souls inspires me. He has let me share just a little in that desire. It is painful at times, but that is the nature of love.

His mercy with me has been limitless. I have often had to say I am sorry, and he has forgiven me, his stubborn follower, repeatedly.

He has given me his mother, Mary, to whom I owe the gift of my vocation, and my perseverance thus far. May she cover me with her mantle and lead me home to Jesus one day.

To summarize, Jesus is my Lord, my God… my faithful friend.

Thank you Jesus. I love you.

Fr. John Bullock, LC

1 John 3:16. All Biblical quotes are taken from the *New American Bible*, Revised Edition 2011, Kindle Edition.

2 *Catechism of the Catholic Church*, 2nd Edition. Vatican: Libreria Editrice Vaticana, 1997, n. 733.

3 Statutes of the Regnum Christi Federation, n. 13, https://www. regnumchristi.org/rcstatutes/wp-content/uploads/2019/06/Statutes-of-the-Regnum-Christi-Federation.pdf.

4 cf. Galatians 4:19.

5 https://www.merriam-webster.com/dictionary/heart.

6 Matthew 7:21, emphasis added.

7 *Christus Vita Vestra: Ratio Institutionis of the Congregation of the Legionaries of Christ*. Rome: Legionaries of Christ, 2017, 228.

8 *Joseph Pearce, Tolkien: Man and Myth: A Literary Life. San Francisco: Ignatius Press, 1998.*

9 Ratzinger, "Message of Fatima." Vatican: Congregation for the Doctrine of the Faith, June 26, 2000.

10 St. John Paul II's definition of "solidarity" is almost interchangeable with love: the decided effort to work for the good of the other.

11 cf. *Catechism of the Catholic Church*, 2nd Edition, n. 33.

12 cf. Bishop Fulton Sheen, *The Way to Inner Peace*. New York: Alba House, 1995 (1st Edition 1949), 185.

13 The Beatles, "All You Need is Love," *Magical Mystery Tour*, 1967.

14 cf. *Compendium of the Catechism of the Catholic Church*. Washington, DC: United States Conference of Catholic Bishops, 2005, n. 358.

15 "Conrad Baars" in Wikipedia, https://en.wikipedia.org/wiki/Conrad Baars.

16 Conrad Baars, MD, *Born Only Once: The Miracle of Affirmation*, 3rd Edition. Eugene, OR: Wipf & Stock, 2016, Kindle Edition, loc. 67.

17 Baars, *Born Only Once…*, 4.

18 Baars, *Born Only Once…*, 12.

19 cf. Baars, *Born Only Once…*, 30.

20 cf. Matthew 22:39.

21 cf. Baars, *Born Only Once…*, 15.

22 Viktor Frankl, *Man's Search for Meaning*. Boston: Beacon Press, 2006, 105, 109.

23 Frankl, *Man's Search for Meaning*, 76.

24 John 12:24

25   Frankl, *Man's Search for Meaning*. Boston: Beacon Press, 2006, xiv.

26   Thomas à Kempis, *The Imitation of Christ*, Book 2, Chapter 3.

27   *Catechism of the Catholic Church*, 2nd Edition, n. 1909.

28   cf. Timothy M. Gallagher, *The Discernment of Spirits: An Ignatian Guide for Everyday Living*, The Crossroad Publishing Co., Kindle Locations 362-363. .

29   cf. Timothy M. Gallagher, *The Discernment of Spirits: An Ignatian Guide for Everyday Living*, The Crossroad Publishing Co., Kindle Locations 362-363.

30   Summa Theologica I, II, 3, 4, and 5 quoted in *Born Only Once…* (Baars), 61.

31   C. S. Lewis, *The Abolition of Man*. New York: MacMillan Company, 1947 (4th printing 1968), 26.

32   Holly Ordway *Not God's Type: An Atheist Academic Lays Down Her Arms*. San Francisco: Ignatius Press, 2014, loc. 454.

33   *Ratio*, 231.

34   cf. Fr. John Bartunek, LC, *Our Formation Pathway: A Regnum Christi Essay on Integral Formation and the Journey to Christian Maturity*. RC Spirituality Center, 2018, Kindle Edition, loc. 577.

35   St. Augustine, *The Works of Saint Augustine: The Confessions of Saint Augustine*. Kindle Edition, 4 (adjusted to contemporary English).

36   John 3:16

37   *Catechism of the Catholic Church*, 2nd Edition, n. 478

38   Romans 5:6.

39   Sally Read. *Night's Bright Darkness: A Modern Conversion Story*. San Francisco: Ignatius Press, 2016, Kindle Edition, Loc. 919.

40   Martin P. Harney, S.J. *The Legacy of Saint Patrick: As Found in His Own Writings*. Boston, MA: St. Paul Editions, 1972, 103-104.

41   Philippians 4:7

42   cf. *Catechism of the Catholic Church*, 2nd Edition , n. 1262.

43   cf. *Catechism of the Catholic Church*, 2nd Edition, n. 1446.

44   Jennifer Fulwiler, *Something Other Than God: How I Passionately Sought Happiness and Accidentally Found It*. San Francisco: Ignatius Press, 2014, 169.

45   Alban Goodier, *Good Galilean*. Sophia Institute Press, 2009. Kindle Edition, loc. 42.

46   He did not need the virtues of faith and hope since he had "knowledge" as the Divine Son.

47   https://www.merriam-webster.com/dictionary/equanimity.

48   cf. Mark 1:34.

49 cf. Mark 6:31.

50 cf. Mark 3:9.

51 cf. Matthew 13:36-43; Luke 6:1-5; Luke 9:54-55; Matthew 16:23.

52 cf. John 2:13-25.

53 Alban Goodier, *The Public Life of Our Lord Jesus Christ: An Interpretation*, v. 2. Originally printed by Kennedy & Sons, 1944 (public domain), Mediatrix Press, 2015, 296.

54 Matthew 26:36-27:56.

55 cf. Luke 22:42-44.

56 *in medio stat virtus*; literally, "virtue stands in the middle," https://worldofdictionary.com/dict/latin-english/meaning/in-medio-stat-virtus.

57 cf. G. K. Chesterton, *Orthodoxy*, (public domain), Kindle version, 36.

58 cf. *Statutes of the Regnum Christi Federation*. May 31, 2019, nn. 20; 25.1; 33.1, 28.1-2.

59 Goodier, *The Public Life of Our Lord Jesus Christ....* v.2, 200.

60 cf. Chesterton, *Orthodoxy*, 85

61 cf. Luke 2:49.

62 cf. Luke 2:49.

63 cf. Matthew 8:10.

64 cf. Matthew 11:25.

65 cf. Matthew 9:36.

66 cf. Matthew 11:21.

67 cf. Mark 10:14.

68 cf. Mark 13:43-44.

69 cf. Luke 9: 37-43.

70 cf. John 11:35.

71 cf. Matthew 26:10-13.

72 cf. Luke 22: 39-46.

73 cf. Luke 22:48.

74 cf. Matthew 26:56; Matthew 27:46.

75 cf. Luke 23:46.

76 https://www.5lovelanguages.com/.

77 cf. John 4:17.

78 Mark 12:34.

79   cf. Matthew 8:11.

80   cf. John 6:20.

81   cf. Luke 8:47.

82   cf. Luke 10:20.

83   Cf. Luke 11:42.

84   cf. Luke 23:39-43.

85   cf. John 6:10.

86   cf. Matthew 4:24.

87   cf. Luke 8:33; Mark 1:26; Matthew 4:25.

88   cf. Matthew 5:1.

89   cf. Luke 8:50.

90   cf. Luke 5:19.

91   cf. Mark 14:22-25.

92   cf. John 19:26-27.

93   cf. John 19:34.

94   cf. John 21:23.

95   cf. John 16:13; Acts 2:2-4.

96   cf. Luke 2:51-52.

97   cf. Luke 2:41-50.

98   cf. John 3:1-21.

99   cf. John 4:1-42.

100 cf. Matthew 9:10.

101 cf. Luke 19:5; Matthew 26:6; John 12:2.

102 cf. Mark 6:31; Mark 4:10.

103 cf. Mark 1:41.

104 cf. Mark 7:33.

105 cf. John 9:6.

106 cf. Matthew 19:15.

107 cf. Luke 8:54.

108 cf. John 20:27.

109 cf. Acts 10:38.

110 John 3:16.

111 Mons. Bougaud, *Jesucristo*. Translated by Doctor E. A. V. Rodriguez.
     Barcelona: Herederos de J. Gili, 1916,. 22-23, my translation from Spanish.

112 cf. Matthew 11:29.

113 cf. Barrs, *Born Only Once*…, 11.

114 cf. John 3:1-15; Matthew 13:1-13; John 18:36-37.

115 Baars, *Born Only Once*…, 22.

116 Matthew 4:10.

117 John 2:17.

118 cf. Mark 3:3-6

119   cf. Mark 1:35.

120 cf. Luke 6:12.

121 cf. Luke 22:44.

122 cf. Mark 6:31.

123 cf. Matthew 8:24

124 John 14:31.

125 John 19:34.

126 Revelation 3:16.

127 Luke 2:49.

128 John 10:30.

129 Matthew 10:32.

130 Matthew 1.1:27.

131 Mark 1:38.

132 John 12:27-28.

133 cf. John 3:16.

134 Luke 15:4-5.

135 Matthew 26:39.

136 Matthew 27:46.

137 Psalms 22:25-28.

138 John 19:30

139 Luke 23:46.

140 Matthew 14:9.

141 John 15:4-5.

142 cf. *Catechism of the Catholic Church*, 2nd Edition, n. 2007.

143 cf. *Catechism of the Catholic Church*, 2nd Edition, n. 1996.

144 cf. *Catechism of the Catholic Church*, 2nd Edition, n. 1127.

145   Luke 22:33-34

146   From the Homily by St. John Chrysostom before he went into exile, tom, iii , p. 415, http://www.todayscatholicworld.com/homily-chrysostom.htm.

147   cf. Matthew 14:14-21.

148   cf. Dallas Jenkins, "What God Told Me about My Failure That Led to 'The Chosen,'" https://www.youtube.com/watch?v=evqanx-4Xpl.

149   James 2:18

150   1 Cor 13:4-7

151   cf. Matthew 7:34

152   Matthew 11:38

153   David B. Morris, "Belief and Narrative," The Scientist, 19 (Sup 1): (March 28, 2005), https://www.the-scientist.com/supplement/belief-and-narrative-48932.

154   Catechism of the Catholic Church, 2nd Edition, n. 1368.

155   cf. Galatians 6:14.

156   Philippians 4:4.

157   cf. "Benjamin Franklin" in Wikipedia, https://en.wikipedia.org/wiki/Benjamin_Franklin#Virtue,_religion,_and_personal_beliefs.

158   Brett and Kate McKay, "Lessons In Manliness: Benjamin Franklin's Pursuit of the Virtuous Life," updated January 6, 2020, https://www.artofmanliness.com/articles/lessons-in-manliness-benjamin-franklins-pursuit-of-the-virtuous-life/.

159   "Lessons In Manliness: Benjamin Franklin's Pursuit of the Virtuous Life"....

160   Statutes of the Regnum Christi Federation, n. 12. https://www.regnumchristi.org/rcstatutes/wp-content/uploads/2019/06/Statutes-of-the-Regnum-Christi-Federation.pdf.

161   Ratzinger, "Message of Fatima," CDF, June 26, 2000.

162   Statutes of the Regnum Christi Federation, n. 13. https://www.regnumchristi.org/rcstatutes/wp-content/uploads/2019/06/Statutes-of-the-Regnum-Christi-Federation.pdf.

163   cf. St. Paul VI, Evangelii Nuntiandi, n. 41.

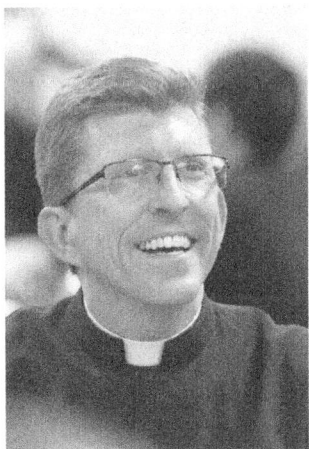

Fr. John Bullock is a priest with the Legionaries of Christ, ordained in 2002. He currently works in Cincinnati, Ohio as a retreat director and spiritual guide for the Regnum Christi Movement. He also serves as an assistant chaplain for the Newman Center at Northern Kentucky University.

You can follow Fr. John Bullock's blog:
https://www.headandheartcatholic.com/

Made in the USA
Monee, IL
17 November 2020